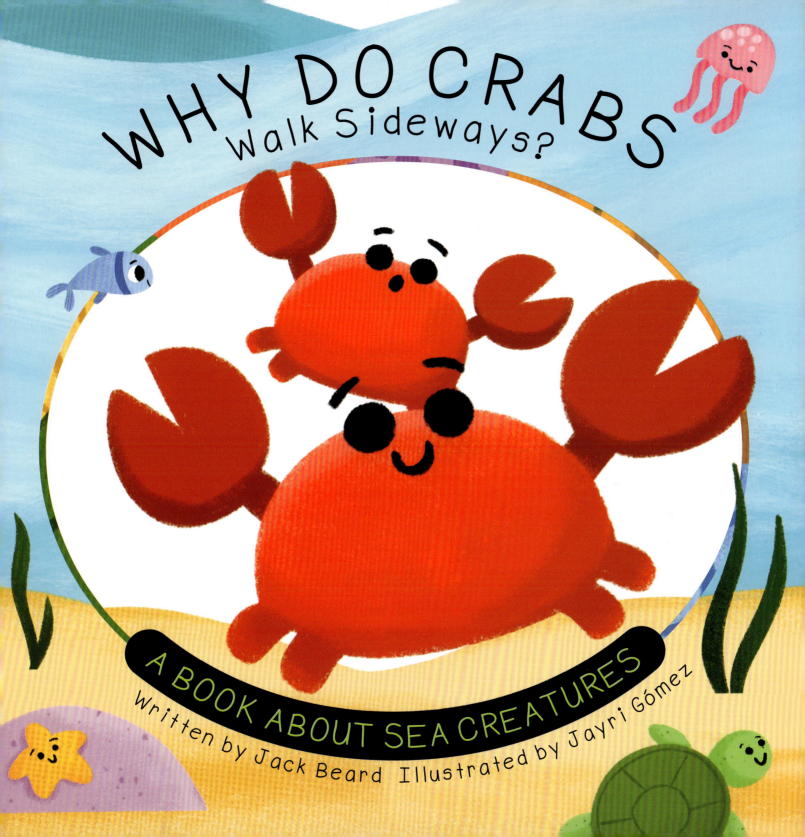

stingray

Have you ever wondered WHY sea creatures do the things they do?

The ocean is home to lots of interesting animals that are fun to see and even more fun to learn about! Each of these creatures have special traits that help them live and thrive in the ocean.

crab

coral

starfish

Is it because they are doing the crab cha-cha?

Crabs walk sideways because of the way their legs are designed. Their joints allow them to move sideways more easily than moving forward.

Can you walk like a crab?

Why don't fish have eyelids?

bubbles

Can you find the fish wearing a hat?

Is it because they are afraid of the dark and don't want to close their eyes?

deep sea anglerfish

How do fish sleep if they can't close their eyes? Fish don't need to close their eyes to sleep. Instead, they slow down their swimming and drift in the water while they rest. Some fish even find a comfy nook in the rocks or plants.

seaweed

Zzz

Can you find the fish sleeping in the seaweed?

Octopuses change color to protect themselves from predators. They will change to blend in with their surroundings. This is called camouflage.

Octopuses have special cells in their skin that are kind of like tiny, stretchy balloons. When an octopus wants to change color, its brain tells the muscles around these cells to tighten or relax, which changes the color.

Octopuses also change colors to talk to other octopuses!

"Hey, Bob! Want to share a crab snack?"

"Nah, I'm busy sorting my shells."

octopus

How many hidden octopuses can you find?

Why do sea turtles look like they are crying?

sea turtle

How many bubbles are on this page?

Sea turtles sometimes get too much salt in their bodies from the ocean water. They get rid of all the extra salt by letting it out of special glands near their eyes. The drops from those glands look like tears.

Why do whales sing to other whales?

Are they auditioning for *This Ocean's Got Talent* to impress their whale friends?

whale

Scientists have discovered that whales use their songs to talk to each other and find other members of their group, also called a pod.

I SWIM FREE
IN THE DEEP BLUE SEA.
BUT IN MY HEART,
I SEARCH FOR THEE...

Whales also sing for their supper. They send out sound waves when they sing. Those waves then bounce back so the whale knows where to find their food.

Can you spot the fish swimming by?

Coral reefs are actually animals! Imagine a coral reef as an underwater city. The base of a coral reef is made up of tiny animals called coral polyps. Each polyp has a short, tube-shaped body. These polyps work together to build a hard external skeleton to protect themselves from danger.

WHAT ELSE CAN SEA CREATURES DO?

There is so much to learn about animals in the sea. Read more about each one here!

SEA TURTLE

Some sea turtles can live up to 100 years!

Sea turtles can lay up to 180 eggs at a time.

Leatherback sea turtles can travel up to 10,000 miles (16,000 km) in a year!

CRAB

Crabs have ten legs. Two of their legs are large claws that are also called pincers.

Crabs can be found in all oceans and even in some fresh water lakes and rivers.

Crabs breathe using gills just like fish!

STARFISH

Starfish aren't fish. They are more closely related to sea cucumbers and sand dollars.

Starfish can live up to 35 years!

Some starfish can grow up to 40 arms.

PUFFERFISH

Pufferfish are sometimes called blowfish.

To get away from predators, pufferfish can blow their bodies up with air or water to several sizes larger than their normal size!

CORAL

Corals eat plankton and even some small fish.

One of the most famous coral reefs is the Great Barrier Reef in Australia. It's 1,429 miles (2,300 km) long!

OCTOPUS

Octopuses have three hearts!

Each arm on an octopus can do different things at the same time. Their arms not only feel things, they can taste and smell them, too.

JELLYFISH

Jellyfish don't have a brain, bones, eyes, or a heart.

Jellyfish eat plants, shrimp, and even crabs.

Some jellyfish can glow in the dark.

BLUE WHALE

Blue whales are the largest animals to ever live on Earth!

Blue whales can grow up to 100 feet (30 m) long!

Blue whales can hear other blue whales up to 1,000 miles (1,609 km) away.

STINGRAY

Stingrays are closely related to sharks.

Some stingrays have venomous barbs in their tails to protect themselves from predators!

Female stingrays are larger than male stingrays.